D1066402

A Blue Banner Biography

Mario

Kathleen Tracy

Mitchell Lane Publishers
P.O. Box 196
Hockessin, Delaware 19707
Visit us on the web: www.mitchelllane.com
Comments? email us: mitchelllane@mitchelllane.com

Copyright © 2006 by Mitchell Lane Publishers. All rights reserved. No part of this book may be reproduced without written permission from the publisher. Printed and bound in the United States of America.

Printing   1   2   3   4   5   6   7   8   9

Blue Banner Biographies

Alicia Keys	Allen Iverson	Ashanti
Ashlee Simpson	Ashton Kutcher	Avril Lavigne
Beyoncé	Bow Wow	Britney Spears
Christina Aguilera	Christopher Paul Curtis	Clay Aiken
Condoleezza Rice	Daniel Radcliffe	Derek Jeter
Eminem	Eve	Ja Rule
Jay-Z	Jennifer Lopez	J. K. Rowling
Jodie Foster	Justin Berfield	Kate Hudson
Lance Armstrong	Lindsay Lohan	**Mario**
Mary-Kate and Ashley Olsen	Melissa Gilbert	Michael Jackson
Missy Elliott	Nelly	P. Diddy
Paris Hilton	Queen Latifah	Rita Williams-Garcia
Ritchie Valens	Ron Howard	Rudy Giuliani
Sally Field	Selena	Shirley Temple
Usher		

Library of Congress Cataloging-in-Publication Data
Tracy, Kathleen.
    Mario / by Kathleen Tracy.
        p. cm. — (A blue banner biography)
    Includes bibliographical references (p.), discography (p.), and index.
    ISBN 1-58415-391-1 (library bound)
    1. Mario, 1987—Juvenile literature. 2. Singers—United States—Biography—Juvenile literature.
I. Title. II. Series.
ML3930.M314T73 2006
782.421643'092—dc22

                                                                            2005014902

ABOUT THE AUTHOR: Kathleen Tracy has been a journalist for over twenty years. Her writing has been featured in magazines including *The Toronto Star*'s "Star Week," *A Biography* magazine, *KidScreen* and *TV Times*. She is also the author of numerous biographies including, *The Boy Who Would be King* (Dutton), *Jerry Seinfeld—The Entire Domain* (Carol Publishing), *Don Imus—America's Cowboy* (Carroll), *William Hewlett: Pioneer of the Computer Age* and *The Fall of the Berlin Wall* both for Mitchell Lane. Also for Mitchell Lane, she wrote *Justin Berfield* and *Lindsay Lohan*. She recently completed *Diana Rigg: The Biography* for Benbella Books.

PHOTO CREDITS: Cover—Jim Cooper/AP Photo; pp. 4, 24—Frank Micelotta/Getty Images; p. 7—Kevin Winter/Getty Images; p. 9—Lawrence Lucier/Getty Images; p. 11—Andrew Holbrooks/ Corbis; p. 17—Larry Busacca/WireImage; p. 19—Chris Polk/AP Photo; p. 22—Theo Wargo/ WireImage; p. 27—John Stanton/Getty Images; p. 29—Michelle Cop/Getty Images.

PUBLISHER'S NOTE: The following story has been thoroughly researched, and to the best of our knowledge, represents a true story. While every possible effort has been made to ensure accuracy, the publisher will not assume liability for damages caused by inaccuracies in the data, and makes no warranty on the accuracy of the information contained herein. This story has not been authorized nor endorsed by Mario Barrett.

Codman Sq. Branch Library
690 Washington Street
Dorchester, MA 02124

MAR - - 2006

CONTENTS

Mario has become one of today's most successful R&B singers. His style is often compared to Usher. In this picture Mario performs while shooting a music video for the song "How Could You" from his second CD, Turning Point.

CHAPTER 1

Meeting an Idol

Even the biggest stars have idols whom they admire. R&B singer Mario Barrett is no exception. As a young child, he would spend hours listening to records by his favorite singers. He was particularly interested in artists who were popular in the 1960s and 1970s, such as the Temptations and the Isley Brothers.

"For me, I have times where I just feel like old music, I don't feel like new music," Mario said in an interview with the *Associated Press*. He explained that he first started listening to older music "to find out what real music is. I'm not that type of artist where I'm just going to say, 'OK, this is what's happening and this is what it is.' It had to be something else, it had to come from somewhere else."

Of all the old performers, his favorite is Stevie Wonder. In fact, sometimes Mario calls himself "Boy Wonder" in honor of his idol. And not only is Stevie Wonder a musical hero, he is a personal inspiration to Mario as well.

Stevie Wonder's real name is Steveland Morris. When he was born he was put in an incubator, which is a container that allows doctors to control temperature. Stevie was accidentally given too much oxygen, which caused him to go blind. Even though he lost his eyesight, Stevie refused to let his disability prevent him from pursuing his love of music. Just like Mario, Stevie knew from a young age he wanted to be a performer. By the time he was five, he could play the harmonica. He started playing the piano at seven. Two years later, he was playing the drums and would play along to music on the radio. Soon, he started writing his own songs.

Just like Mario, Stevie knew from a young age he wanted to be a performer. By the time he was five, he could play the harmonica. He started playing piano at seven.

When his family moved to Detroit, even more people recognized his talent. People were so impressed with Stevie's musical abilities that they asked him to perform at his local church. Detroit was the home of Motown, a famous record label. A family friend took eleven-year-old Stevie to audition for the owner of the record label, who immediately signed him to a record deal and gave him the stage name Little Stevie Wonder. Within two years, he had a number one record called "Fingertips." More than forty years later, he is still one of the world's most respected and influential musicians and performers.

One of Mario's idols while growing up was Stevie Wonder, who went blind shortly after he was born. Like Mario, Wonder started performing as a young boy. Today, he is considered one of the most influential musicians of the 20th century. Mario says meeting Stevie Wonder at a party was one of the highlights of his life.

When Mario had the opportunity to meet Stevie Wonder in February 2002 during the Grammy Awards, he was thrilled. Mario was invited to attend a party at the house of Clive Davis. Davis is the founder of Arista, which is Mario's record label. Barrett told TeenPeople.com that it was overwhelming to see so many famous performers.

Since 2001, Mario has had many dreams come true. He's had a number one record. . . . He's won awards. He's become famous.

"Everybody was there. Janet [Jackson], my man Justin Timberlake—I call him by his last name. We sat right across from each other, and he told me that he thought I would last a long time in the game."

But most amazing to Mario was that Stevie Wonder was there. Davis asked Mario to sing, so Mario chose one of Wonder's songs called "You and I." Stevie was so impressed that he spent time talking to Mario and giving him advice. But more exciting was that Stevie wanted to work with Mario. "He told me that he wanted to do some songs on my next album. That would be *crazy*. I would love to do something like that—it would be a dream come true."

Since 2001, Mario has had many dreams come true. He's had a number-one record. He's gotten to travel all over the world. He's won awards. He's become famous. Through it all, Mario has tried to keep his success in perspective, and he still wants to follow in the footsteps of his musical role model.

"I always want to be known first of all as a humble person, God-fearing," Mario revealed in a Langfield Entertainment online interview. "Next, I want to be known as a real true artist. You know how they still talk about Sam Cooke, Marvin Gaye, Al Green and Stevie Wonder? That's how I want to be remembered."

So far, he seems well on his way to fulfilling that dream, too.

Mario's talent was obvious from the time he was a toddler. Despite all his success, though, he says he wants people to know that he's a religious and humble person. His goal is to have as long and respected a career as classic artists like Marvin Gaye, Al Green, and Stevie Wonder.

CHAPTER 2

Born to Perform

Since the city was established in 1729, Baltimore, Maryland, has been one of America's busiest ports. That's because it lies farther west than any other major Atlantic port. The city is perhaps best known as the place where Francis Scott Key wrote "The Star-Spangled Banner." He wrote the song after watching American soldiers at Fort McHenry defend Baltimore from attack by the British during the War of 1812.

Considering its historic musical past, it seems fitting that Mario Barrett calls Baltimore home. He was born there on August 27, 1986. His mother, Shawntia Hardaway, was a single parent who worked hard to provide a comfortable home.

In an interview with Calvin Terrell, Mario said that, growing up, he didn't spend as much time with his siblings as he would have liked. "It was just me at home but I have four sisters and one brother on my father's side I saw growing up here and there. We're a lot closer now than we were before because when I got a chance to get out on my

The first time Mario's mom, Shawntia Hardaway, heard him sing she thought it was a song playing on the radio. Mario says his mom has been his biggest supporter and his biggest inspiration. Unable to afford music lessons for her son, she bought him a karaoke machine so he could learn songs.

own I went back [to] spend time with my brother and sisters." Mario now also has two brothers "on my mother's side that are both younger than me."

Mario says that from his earliest memories, he wanted to be a singer, a dream his mother actively encouraged. She would frequently play the piano and have her son sing along with her. When he was just four years old, Hardaway realized how much natural talent Mario had.

Mario says that from his earliest memories, he wanted to be a singer, a dream his mother actively encouraged.

"I was downstairs in my house barely dressed wearing mismatching shoes. My mother heard me singing," the singer told WVCR.com. "When she came downstairs she was shocked when she realized that it was me."

Hardaway confirms his story. "I walked down the steps and I said, 'Oh my god, that's Mario singing,' " she recalled to writer Cheryl Lu-Lien Tan. "My friend said, 'Oh, Shawn, that's the radio,' and I said, 'No, it's my baby. It's Mario!' "

She immediately went out and bought Mario a karaoke machine and encouraged him to sit at the piano and tap out melodies. Hardaway also made sure Mario had plenty of music from which to learn. "If it wasn't for her keeping music in my ear, like Stevie Wonder, Marvin Gaye, Donny Hathaway, Usher and people like that, I wouldn't be doing this now," Mario told BET.com.

They couldn't afford for Mario to have private vocal lessons, but he was able to learn just from listening to music. "I've had no voice training whatsoever; just practice and listening to good music," he revealed in a DotMusic.com interview. "My mother kept playing music and kept musical instruments around me while I was growing up, and that's how I fell in love with music."

Mario feels the education his mother provided was just as beneficial as going to a class would have been. "I played with the tools that she had given me and went for broke!" he recalled. "From that experience I have learned to create and develop harmonies by just listening to the melodies. My mother and father can both sing, but I'm the only one that really pursued it. I can't really say that I got it from any of them but I can say I got it from practicing a lot and sticking with it."

"My mother kept playing music and kept musical instruments around me while I was growing up, and that's how I fell in love with music."

Although all of his family supported him, Mario says only his mother understood how serious he was about making a career of singing. "That's why she was my inspiration."

While in Bedford Elementary School, Mario started performing at church, in school talent contests, and even at the barber shop. "I would go to get my hair cut and my mom would tell me to sing for the customers," he recalled to MSNBC. "All the dudes would give me a couple dollars, and I really thought I was doing something. That's when I realized that singing was what I wanted to do."

When he was eleven, he started signing up for local singing competitions. Rather than rap or perform hip-hop,

Mario sang the ballad "I'll Make Love to You" by Boyz II Men. He won several of the contests. It was through one such contest that Mario got his first break.

A talent show host named Anthony Jeter selected Mario to be in a competition held at Baltimore's Dunbar High School. In the audience that night was a manager named Troy Patterson. After watching his performance, Patterson contacted Jeter and asked him to drive Mario to his office in New Jersey for a meeting.

Impressed by the young man's talent and ambition, [Troy] Patterson agreed to start managing Mario.

Impressed by the young man's talent and ambition, Patterson agreed to start managing Mario. He arranged for him to join a four-member group. One of the other boys was the son of actress Mo'Nique. The group began performing at talent shows. Ironically, the boys sang the same Boyz II Men song that Mario had sung before in contests.

It didn't take Mario long to realize that he was better suited for performing alone. He went back to pursuing a career as a solo artist. A short time later, one of the most legendary producers in music would change Mario's life.

CHAPTER 3

A Golden Opportunity

Troy Patterson never doubted that Mario was destined for stardom. "I'd never heard an eleven-year-old sing that well," he said to the Baltimore *Sun* newspaper. "There are a lot of people out there right now who have talent, people who sing, who are professionals, who sing live and sing out of key. Some sing flat and some sing sharp, but he didn't have that problem. He has an incredible ear, and that is impressive. To be eleven years old and stand up there like you've been doing this all your life pretty much already, he just has a natural, God-given talent. I thought, 'This could be the next big thing out of Baltimore.' "

When he wasn't in school at Milford Mill Academy, Mario continued to work on his singing. At times he wondered if he would ever get the chance to finally prove himself. "Growing up in Baltimore for me was hard at times," Mario admitted to the *Sun*. "I was going through a lot, hanging out on the street sometimes, doing things I wasn't supposed to be doing. Just being out late, stuff like that. I wasn't doing, like, crazy things.

"But every day on the street you had dudes selling drugs, and I even had friends who were into it," he said. "I wasn't trying to be someone like that, but I think, because every day, I was seeing the same thing, my eyes were shut to the outside world. But when I got away, I got a chance to see the world."

When Mario was fifteen, Patterson believed his client was ready to turn professional. He set up a meeting with producer Clive Davis.

When Mario was fifteen, Patterson believed his client was ready to turn professional. He set up a meeting with producer Clive Davis, the founder of Arista Records and a member of the Rock and Roll Hall of Fame. Davis had launched the careers of many singers, including Bruce Springsteen and Whitney Houston. However, despite his legendary status, Mario had no real idea who Davis was, so he was not nervous to meet him. At least not at first.

"I went in the office, and he's talking on his phone, and his office looked like out of this planet," he recalled to writer Cheryl Lu-Lien Tan. "Man, it was so beautiful. Then I was very nervous, because I'd seen that office, and I knew he had to be somebody to have an office like that."

Mario had no reason to worry. After listening to him sing, Davis—now running J Records—offered the teenager

Clive Davis is a legendary record producer. He is the founder of Arista Records. Among the artists he's worked with are Bruce Springsteen and Whitney Houston. Davis signed Mario to a contract after having him sing in his office.

a contract. "I think his exact words were, 'We at J Records would love to have you on this label.' I didn't really catch it until I went home, and then I thought, 'Man, this could be a turning point or something. This is my dream, what I wanna do.' "

Mario told SoulTrain.com that he got even more excited the more he learned about Davis's career. "He's the best; he's the top of the game right now. He made Alicia Keys blow up like crazy. She was just doing talent shows with her band. Clive took her under his wing and just made her fly away. He's definitely doing big things. Clive's got a lot of energy in him. He's ready to do anything to make his artist huge."

But in order to get his chance at success, Mario would have to make a big sacrifice. He would have to move away from home. He went to live with Patterson in Teaneck, New Jersey, where he was tutored at home for four hours a day. Meanwhile, he began working on various projects. He performed on the song "Tameeka" that appeared on the *Dr. Dolittle 2* movie sound track. Davis also took him to a post-Grammy party, where he got to meet many of the singers he grew up listening to. The experience made Mario work even harder.

Davis teamed Mario with many experienced R&B producers and songwriters, including Alicia Keys, who wrote two songs for the album.

Not long after, he started working on his first album. Davis teamed Mario with many experienced R&B producers and songwriters, including Alicia Keys, who wrote two songs for the album. She also took the time to give the young singer some advice. "Alicia is a very sweet person, and she showed me a lot of love," he recalled in an interview with Bret McCabe. "She was just trying to help me out, telling me how everything was going to be crazy and that there was going to be a lot of stress with that, but to have fun doing it at the same time. You know, this is my job now."

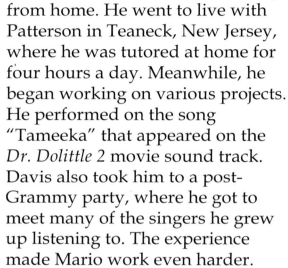

Just before the release of his first album, Mario was asked by SoulTrain.com if he worried about living up to all the expectations. "Not really. I figure everything is going to be cool. I don't know how everybody is going to react to the album. But I'm trying to be very realistic about everything. Take it as it comes. I can't do nothing else but be me."

And that would prove to be more than enough.

Many successful producers and writers want to work with Mario. Grammy-winning singer Alicia Keys (shown here) wrote two songs for Mario's first album. Barrett says Keys has become like a sister to him.

CHAPTER 4

A Successful Debut

Mario's first album, called *Mario,* entered the *Billboard* Top 200 album chart in the number nine spot. In the same week the first single, "Just a Friend 2002," was number five. Not only were fans raving about Mario, but so were critics. They were particularly impressed with his voice and natural air when performing.

"I didn't know people would accept it," he admitted later in a *Sacramento Observer* interview. "God was on my side and I thank him every day for the blessing."

But Mario would discover that releasing the album was only the first part of being a successful recording artist. Promoting his music would be just as important. Promoting would involve equal parts incredible fun and hard work. Shortly after the release of the album, Mario went on tour. He performed as the opening act for rap artist Bow Wow. Next, he participated in the Scream 3 Tour.

At times life on the road was a strain. "I don't get much time to be a kid," he once commented to SoulTrain.com.

"Definitely my childhood has been taken away from me, not being able to go out with my friends and doing what I want, not being able to go to regular school."

When he did have some free time, Mario was just like any other teenager. "I have a thing for PlayStation and I'm really competitive," he told WVCR.com. "When I'm not doing that, I'm getting together with my friends and talking or playing football." But most of the time Mario was performing.

When he did have some free time, Mario was just like any other teenager. "I have a thing for PlayStation and I'm really competitive."

The teenager thoroughly enjoyed the adoration of his fans, although suddenly being recognized in public "was overwhelming" and took some getting used to. "I love it. It's not as stressful as you think. You just gotta buckle down and you know that whatever you do, your fans love you. And if they don't scream for you, they don't love you as much."

Sometimes his fans love him a little too much. "I had on a pair of basketball tear-away pants that were too big," he recalled to *Ebony*. "In the front row these girls started pulling at my legs, and all of a sudden my pants fell down. I was so embarrassed! But I just pulled them back up, got through the song and changed my pants."

While the kind of success he was enjoying might have gone to his head, Mario was careful to stay grounded. "You can't help it getting to you, but you can't let it take over. I

Mario says his fans recognize him wherever he goes. He enjoys talking to his fans and hearing what they think about his music. During a concert one time, so many fans were reaching for him that they accidentally pulled his pants down.

get my alone time to try to balance it out," he told the *Sacramento Observer*.

The second single from his debut album turned Mario into a teen heartthrob. Called "Braid My Hair," the song was a ballad that the singer told *Teen Scream* reflected his homesickness. "It's basically talking about being on the road, missing home, and how sometimes I just want to go home and chill with my girl and have her braid my hair."

Suddenly, Mario became known as much for his own cornrow-style braids as for his singing.

As his fame grew, so did the number of people who wanted to be his friend. Mario has been careful not to mistake real friends for people who just want to be around somebody famous. "The only real people are the people that have been there from the beginning," he cautions. Everybody else will definitely be nice to you, but I wouldn't say they are fake; I just wouldn't say all my business to them or be really personal to them."

Unlike so many other young stars who suddenly find themselves famous with a lot of money, Mario was proud of being known as a wholesome performer.

Unlike so many other young stars who suddenly find themselves famous with a lot of money, Mario was proud of being known as a wholesome performer. He told *Ebony* that he's never been pressured by friends to do anything he didn't want to do. "I'm my own person, so it doesn't matter what people do around me. I think that's because I always listen to my mother's advice. She has never been wrong, whether it's about the business or the streets."

Mario's album would sell more than half a million copies in the United States alone. He had a loyal following of fans and the respect of critics. But instead of recording another album immediately, Mario took a two-year break from music. When he made his return, the teenage singer was all grown up.

During the two-year break he took from music, Mario's appearance underwent a big change. Although he became famous for having his hair braided, now Mario prefers a more sophisticated look. He is also taller and more interested in fashionable clothes. Most importantly, his voice changed—for the better.

CHAPTER 5

Mario Grows Up

Just when his career was taking off, Mario surprised everyone by taking a two-year break. He would later explain that there were several reasons for the layoff. First, he wanted to finish high school, which he did in 2004. Next, he felt he needed to take a step back and absorb everything that had happened to him. "The thing that I've really noticed is that I'm starting to understand what it really means to appreciate family, people, relationships, my fans and life," he said in a Delafont.com chat. "The success I had was so unexpected. I didn't really get a chance to think about it before."

But the main reason for the extended time off was to wait for his voice to stop changing. "It was scary," he admitted to *People*. "I thought I was losing my voice."

To his relief, just the opposite happened. By the time he graduated, Mario's voice matured and sounded even better than before. Meanwhile, the singer had changed in other ways, too. He was taller, had cut off his braids, and was dressing more like a fashion model than a scooter-riding high-school kid. In other words, Mario had come of age. His new album, released in 2004, reflected that.

"On my last album I was really introducing myself to the world," he explained to writer Calvin Terrell. "Nobody really knew me but my mother. So on this album I had to introduce the fact that I've grown up, I'm changing and I'm on my journey to manhood. That's the reason it's called *Turning Point*."

"... It means a lot to me to do something I love. It's not about the money. It's not about the fame. It's really about the love for it."

Mario also pointed out that the changes weren't just in his appearance. "Now I also have more control over what I'm doing. I'm focused and determined to achieve my dream, more understanding of what it means to be an artist, what it means to be a singer, what it means to give a good show, what it means to love somebody. All these things play a part in who I am. It means a lot to me to be able to do something I love. It's not about the money. It's not about the fame. It's really about the love for it."

And there is nothing he loves more than performing live. According to the *Sarasota Herald-Tribune*, Mario said, "You can show people who you really are and you get to show your talent by singing live." He later told Calvin Terrell, "I get very emotional before I do my shows because me being on stage singing means more than just a show; it's my life."

The new album was an immediate hit and sold over a million copies in a matter of months. The first single spent ten weeks as the number one song in America. Even though Mario says the album simply reflects who he is, his singing style made many people compare him to another R&B singer: Usher. Although Mario is flattered at the comparison, he is quick to point out they are each distinct individuals.

Singing is more than just a job to Mario. He doesn't sing to be famous or to make a lot of money. He sings because he loves it. Mario has often been compared to singer Usher.

"I have so much respect for the guy," he told *Ebony*. "But I am trying to go about things differently with my music. There will never be another Usher. There will never be another Mario."

Mario acknowledged to Calvin Terrell that it may surprise some people to know he is very religious. He explained, "My mother is very religious. She passed that down to me. I'm very appreciative about my life, about the vision that God gives me. I think that God only gives that to certain people who really appreciate it. So I just try to show my appreciation by being humble, working and being positive about what I do. The music industry opens many doors for you. After the next couple singles, I'll try and do some acting and cameos. All I can do is try my best and work my hardest."

"I'm letting everybody know that I'm creative, controversial and not stuck on one thing. I'm ready to do it all."

In 2005, when *Ebony* asked where he hopes to be in five years, Mario admitted he has his sights set on much more than just music. "At twenty-three, I would like to have a movie or two and my fourth album coming out around the same time, and my own record label."

Whatever happens, Mario feels ready for it. On his official Web site he assured his fans, "I'm letting everybody know that I'm creative, controversial and not stuck on one thing. I'm ready to do it all."

Although singing is his first love, Mario would also like to try acting as well as music producing. His dream is to have a long, successful career and believes if you work hard enough, you can achieve all your dreams.

CHRONOLOGY

1986	Mario Barrett is born August 27.
1990	His mother buys him a karaoke machine.
1997	Mario begins performing in singing competitions. Troy Patterson becomes Mario's manager.
2001	Clive Davis signs Mario to a record deal.
2002	His first album, *Mario,* is released.
2004	Mario graduates from high school. His second album, *Turning Point,* is released.
2005	"Let Me Love You" is the number one song in the country for 10 weeks.

DISCOGRAPHY

2002	*Mario*
2004	*Turning Point*

FOR FURTHER READING

Articles

"Is Mario the New Usher?"
http://groups.msn.com/B2KDotCom2004/mariosister2sisterinterview.msnw

"Mario Tops the Charts with New Song, Style"
http://www.msnbc.msn.com/id/6790192/

"Mario's Turning Point"
http://www.langfieldentertainment.com/MARIO1.htm

Save Our Soul, Artist of the Month: "Mario"
http://www.saveoursoul.nl/aomoct2002/

"Teen Idol Mario Answers Five Questions"
http://www.onlineshawnee.com/stories/112802/you_106.shtml

"Teen Scream: Baltimore's Mario Climbs the Pop Charts"
http://citypaper.com/music/review.asp?rid=7151

On the Internet

Official Web Site
http://www.mario2u.com

J Records
http://www.jrecords.com

INDEX